Shifting I.T. from Technologies to a Business Services Enabler

Mini-Book Strategy Series – Book 6

Authors:
Rand Morimoto, Ph.D.
Rich Dorfman, MBA

Copyright © 2018 Rand Morimoto

All rights reserved.

ISBN: 1985733196
ISBN-13: 978-1985733190

DEDICATION

I dedicate this book to my mother Vickie. Thanks mom for sharing your drive and spirit with your grandkids!
-- Rand

I dedicate this book to my wife Sherry. Thanks Sherry for being a great inspiration and role model!
-- Rich

TABLE OF CONTENTS

Mini-Book Strategy Series – Book 6 i
Dedication iii
Table of Contents v
Introduction vi
1 Leaping Forward: Setting the Vision of a Business Services Focused
I.T. Operations 11
    Different Organizations, Different Strategies 11
    I.T. as a Business Enabler in Retail Sales 12
    I.T. as a Business Enabler in Manufacturing 13
    I.T. as a Business Enabler in Finance 14
    I.T. as a Business Enabler in Healthcare 14
    Creating Business Efficiencies by Leveraging Technical Solutions 15
    Understanding the Focus on the Timing of Innovation to Business
    Enablement 15
    Evolving Clarification of the Value I.T. Brings to an Enterprise 16
2 Understanding the Legacy of I.T. Operations 17
    Tech as a New Resource in the Marketplace 17
    Rethinking Entire Business Processes in a Matter of Years 18
    Decision Making Based on an Emerging Market Mentality 18
    Working Hard to Get Early Tech Working 19
    The Entire Introduction of Technologies in a Single Lifespan 20
3 Cloud Computing Changing the Focus of I.T. to Applications and
Services 21
    Modernizing Applications and Datacenter Operations 21
    The Rise of Shadow I.T. 22
    Leveraging Cloud Computing for Business Application Access 22
    Introduction of Rolling Updates to Enterprise Applications 23
    Selectively Leveraging Cloud Application to Fulfill Business Needs...23
    Changing Business Operations in the Era of Cloud Computing 24
4 Cloud-based Applications and Services as a Transition State 27
    Transitioning I.T. Operations to a Cloud Computing Model 27
    On-premise Administration and Managements Models Inefficient for
    Cloud-based Applications 28
    Applying Archaic Management Models to Modern Application
    Systems 29
    The Need to Backup Cloud-based Data 31
    The Need to Modernize I.T. Operations 32
5 Rethinking I.T. Security and I.T. Operations 33
    Exploits Through the Side Door, not the Front Door 33
    The Logical Solution to the Security Problem 34
    What Change is Necessary? 34
    Why is Time of Essence? 35

Latest Version versus Latest Patches 35
Security is Only as Strong as the Weakest Link 36
What Can be Done to Improve Network Security? 36
How to Minimize Interruption to Critical Business Applications in the New World of Thinking? 37
What About Highly Regulated Systems that Can't be Upgraded so Frequently? 38
Back to the Inconvenience Factor 38

6 Accepting the New Model of Operating Systems and Applications as Services 39
Assessing the Enterprises Shift to Modern Solutions and Services 39
Understanding Modern Methods of Monitoring Modern Applications (monitoring service (user access), not servers/systems, monitoring functional states (send/receive) 40
Shifting Modern Administration to Meet the Needs of Cloud-based Application Models 40
Leveraging Early Fast, Early Slow, and Other New Release Options .40
Rethinking New Feature Enablement, Not Old Function Compatibility 41

7 Developing Split Models for Applications and Services 43
Accepting Dual or Multi-Method Administration and Management ..43
Dual Model for Administration and Management Does Mean More Complexity 45
Modern Systems Requiring More Simplified Models of Management 46
Embracing Management as a Service Model for I.T. Operations 46
More Modern Applications, Minimization of I.T. Time for Mundane Tasks 47
Reshaping I.T. to Focus on Effective Business Services 48

8 Business Services Focused on Revenue Generating Activities 49
Case Scenario – Redistributing Inventory Based on Projected Needs 49
Case Scenario – Providing Necessary Resources In Times of Emergency Needs 50
Case Scenario – Shifting from Blanket Marketing Campaigns to Targeted Sales Campaigns 51
Case Scenario – Making Better Financial Decisions Based on Real time Information 51

9 Business Services Focused on Optimizing Business Operations 53
Case Scenario – Optimizing Transactions for Cost Efficient Models .53
Case Scenario – Leveraging Analytics to Optimize Social Media Outcomes 54
Case Scenario – Improving Healthcare Services through Real Time Communications 55
Case Scenario – Utilizing Predictive Analytics to Accelerate Solution

    Availability 55
10 Wrap-up 57
    Value of Current Knowledge Not Historical Expertise 57
    Importance of Institutional Knowledge 58
    Changing the Mindset to New and Creative Manners of Action 58
    Shifting From Technology Focused to Business Solution Focused 59
About the Authors 61

INTRODUCTION

Over the past 5-10 years, Information Technology (I.T.) has undergone dramatic changes. The evolution of "cloud computing", more employees "bringing your own device" (BYOD) to work, and the immersion of "social media" representing clear signs that I.T is no longer just for techies. The enablement of communications and more readily accessible information fosters collaborative decision-making and improved business processes and operations. As a result, there's a constant demand on I.T. for faster, better, less costly, and more reliable service delivery.

In our two previous books (The New World of I.T & Adapting to the New World of I.T., books 1 & 5 of this series), we detail out the core changes in the needs, expectations, and requirements of a more tech savvy workforce, leveraging that savviness to empower the workforce to do better and greater things through the leveraging of technology, as well as providing prescriptive step by step guidance on how to make this shift – in many cases requiring changes in policies and processes based on best practices from real world experiences. The new reality is that true success can only be measured when transforming I.T. into a business enabler and contributing to the success of the business. Only when I.T. can associate with increases in profitability, be it increased top-line growth, cost reduction, or decreased risk, can I.T. be deemed successful.

INTRODUCTION

The difference between a technology solution provider and a business service enabler is whether I.T. is continuing to "do things" behind the scenes in serving an organization's business needs, or whether I.T. is truly out front directly increasing business revenues and impacting business efficiencies. When I.T. is serving the latter where its services are directly improving the organization's bottom-line, then I.T.'s role has evolved to be a critical business service benefiting the organization.

This book leaps forward to share a glimpse of the state of what I.T. does when it fulfills a Business Services-focused role in an organization, and then works its way back to the integral steps organizations must take in transforming from a technology and solution-focused operation into the business services focused environment. Understanding the legacy model of I.T. Operations, where it currently is and how it got there, is important to making this shift to something new. As we'll address in this book, the hardest part in making the transition to the modern state is changing the culture, the thinking, the years of developed and practiced processes of employees to new and different routines.

1 LEAPING FORWARD: SETTING THE VISION OF A BUSINESS SERVICES FOCUSED I.T. OPERATIONS

Rather than "starting from the beginning" and slowly building the framework of the end state of I.T. operations, we're going to leap forward and provide the vision of what a mature, fully transformed I.T. operations looks like that is serving the business needs of the organization. With this vision in mind, the balance of this book then goes back through the steps and helps walk the reader through the progression of morphing from a traditional legacy-based I.T. operations to a modern "new world" environment.

Different Organizations, Different Strategies

Organizations have a clear focus of what they do, what customers they serve, and the type of business and industry they are in. Retail organizations that sell clothes, shoes, sporting goods, or toys provide their goods to end customers. Someone walks in (or these days may visit a Website), peruses the goods, places what they want in a cart (whether a physical cart of virtual cart), and checks-out by paying for what they want.

LEAPING FORWARD: SETTING THE VISION OF A BUSINESS SERVICES FOCUSED I.T. OPERATIONS

A manufacturer of goods may not serve an end customer directly, but instead be focused at efficiently and effectively producing goods from raw materials, assembling goods, and packaging the goods for transport to distribution and point of sale.

An investment banking firm may not deal with physical products at all, but instead focus on delivering information and services to its end customers. The goal of the investment banking firm isn't to deliver a physical end good, but to complete profitable transactions and provide clear communications and reporting to its end customers.

A hospital does not have discrete products per se nor does it directly provide services, but instead is a gathering place where health-related products and services are provided. Beyond the services it offers, a major focus of the hospital is to be located in a location that can best serve its end customers, whether close to its customers like in the middle of a city, close to a transportation hub such as by a train station, or in a location that has ample parking and easy access that both service providers and end customers can access easily.

Organizations are different, industry to industry, in what they provide and the method in which it fulfills on its role to its end customers; so there's not a single method of delivery or single mode of service for each organization. However each organization has a clear end focus, whether it is to provide direct goods to its customers, to efficiently manufacturer and transport its goods to market, to provide a specific service where communications and reporting is most important, or merely be a meeting place where goods and services are provided. The value of each organization is to fulfill on its role to ultimately care for its end customer as efficiently and effectively as possible.

I.T. as a Business Enabler in Retail Sales

For I.T. operations that are truly acting as business enablers for their organization, the work of I.T. is providing services that address the end goals of the organization.

For a retailer that is focused on providing goods directly to the end customers, I.T.'s ability to make the goods visually available to customers, help facilitate answers to questions that buyers may commonly ask, efficiently get the buyers' goods checked-out, and help the end customer to properly use and ultimately enjoy or gain value from the purchase.

The reason Amazon.com has been so successful as a seller of products isn't just because it provides users a method of selecting goods and having them delivered to them within a couple days, but users can quickly and easily search for a product, read about the product, see comparisons between the product and competing options, read reviews from other buyers about the product, and quickly make the self-selection that the product is what they are looking for. Amazon provides videos and links to manuals, usage directions, and guidance on how a product is used; and it provides an easy method for users to return products if the item doesn't work or they're not satisfied with it. Even when a customer cannot return an item, Amazon's feedback and review process at least allows a customer to complain about the product and to advise others not to buy the product, which for buyers isn't as good as actually getting a refund for something they don't want or doesn't work, but at least the buyer can gain comfort that others won't make the same purchase. Further, the mere fact that the buyer has the ability to influence future sales provides them enough leverage, that in most cases, the seller is motivated to just provide a refund. Bottom-line, Amazon makes the purchase process simple, helps its buyers successfully use the product, and provides its buyers a method to resolve problems or concerns with the products purchased.

I.T. as a Business Enabler in Manufacturing

Manufacturing organizations can benefit from I.T.'s services by having I.T. improve efficiencies in moving raw materials from place to place, improving efficiencies in the direct manufacturing and assembling of goods, and quickly get the finished goods to the buyer of the goods. I.T.'s role in manufacturing is to help minimize production and transportation times, making sure the right item, is in the right place, at the right time.

Manufacturing efficiencies benefit from the use of "data". Knowing what, needs to be where, and when, and then controlling those times and materials movement are the important factors. Moving too many items is inefficient as it takes more transport and storage resources to move goods from one place to another. However, not moving enough raw materials means that a manufacturing run could be completed without a sufficient number of items produced. Take the example of just in time manufacturing processes that may require retooling between batches. If a machine is loaded up with yellow paint and it takes half a day to clean the machine to change paint colors, unless we produce enough goods that makes it efficient to incur a half day of downtime to change colors, then the manufacturer risks overproducing stock that doesn't sell fast enough.

When I.T. can leverage current and historical data to predict appropriate production quantities, move the optimal amount of raw materials, and instruct systems to manufacture the right amount of goods to meet demand, then I.T. has achieved its role as a business enabler in facilitating efficient and cost-effective manufacturing.

I.T. as a Business Enabler in Finance

I.T.'s role in finance could also be about moving banking goods (cash, coins) from place to place. However, in the era of digital transactions, it's less about product movement and more about information. At the heart of the finance industry is information, the ledger that holds the information of what the end customer has that the financial institution owes its customer. It's about leveraging assets so that the funds being held can be used to grow in value, rather than to remain idle and unused. It's about sharing with the end customer other services provided by the organization that the customer can take advantage of, expanding the role of services that the institution can provide to its end customers.

In the finance and banking industry, it's about "data" as well. It's about efficiently and effectively retaining records of transactions so that the right owner of assets and all transactions are properly retained. Data helps decision-makers leverage market information to make informed decisions so that assets are leveraged in the right manner benefiting the institution and its customers. The ability for the organization to share the latest information, the products and services offered, and how it extends its value and to its end customers are the key enablers of I.T.'s benefit to the finance organization.

I.T. as a Business Enabler in Healthcare

For healthcare, the business enabler that I.T. provides is also focused around data: keeping track of health records and ensuring that the resources needed to provide health services are available, in the right place, at the right time, in the right quantities. It's more than just tracking patient data, but ensuring that the resources needed to provide the right health services to the needs and demands of its patients are fulfilled.

Data can be best leveraged by more than simply checking patients in and out of the facility, but forecasting trends, assessing current outbreaks, leveraging predictions on upcoming weather trends that may suggest a higher (or lower) need for health professionals, vaccines, medical supplies, and materials needed to fulfill on an anticipated and modeled analysis of needs in advance of the organization's actual needs.

I.T. can help a healthcare organization not merely be reactive to demand for services, but provide predictive and prescriptive analytical assessment to move needed supplies and resources to the right location in anticipation of needs and then reshift resources as the needs of the organization change.

Creating Business Efficiencies by Leveraging Technical Solutions

Utilizing data analytics to produce products more efficiently, decrease selling time, to improve collaboration and communications, shorten the sales and manufacturing cycles are just a few examples of the way that technology can be used for to improve business efficiencies. The better that demand can be predicted and resources managed ahead of time to fulfill on the need, the better the organization can take advantage of the spurt in needs that may result in increased sales or simply ensuring goods and services are available when needed.

Data can also help an organization prevent / minimize over-buying or over-producing goods that will eventually need to be disposed of, minimizing loss and waste. Even where an organization may need to dispose of goods, rather than going through a warehouse months later to determine that the organization has an excess of expired goods that has to be disposed of at a loss, if the organization had a good tracking of the goods and expiration dates of the goods, the older materials may potentially have been rotated into use in other sites. Goods that are identified as excess before expiration can potentially be sold or transported to an organization or area that could use the materials, even if it means the organization may have to donate the goods, better to rotate the goods to be used by charity than to be destroyed after an expiration date.

Understanding the Focus on the Timing of Innovation to Business Enablement

Some may argue that I.T. has always been a business enabler, with email improving communications, Client Relationship Management systems improving client retention, shared document stores eliminating lengthy communications cycles. True, when mailing customer proposals gave way to faxing proposals to near instantaneous email exchange of documentation, the communications cycle went from days to seconds. But these technologies were put in place 5, 10, 20 years ago and the efficiencies from those technologies have already been absorbed into the business operations stream. It would be like a race car organization saying their car is super-fast and efficient because of this concept call the wheel invented hundreds of years ago.

Business Enablement of I.T. is about the creative invention and modern development of ideas, use of technologies, and strategies leveraging the latest technologies available in the marketplace that have a direct impact on the frontline of an organization in new and creative ways. It's about developing new strategies and leveraging the latest in technological inventions that can help an organization create a competitive advantage that is unique in the marketplace, and constantly innovating technological solutions to keep the enterprise at the peak of its abilities and efficiencies.

Evolving Clarification of the Value I.T. Brings to an Enterprise

There has been repeated use of the term Direct Impact as the importance in business enablement and the shift from being just backend focused to being more impactful on frontline activities. By backend, we refer to technologies like storage systems, compute systems, and databases that are still extremely important in I.T.'s role in providing an enterprise the core resources it needs to leverage technology for its benefit. But, these backend tools shouldn't define I.T. as its core value anymore. It's like attributing a hammer or tape measure as a contractor's primary value in creating a skyscraper. While those tools are important in the construction of a building, it's the use of many other materials, such as leveraging load bearing structures that make up the entire structure that occupants of the building can utilize.

With the expansion of cloud computing, many tools can be purchased on an hourly or monthly basis. In most cases, the building contractor is better off leasing the huge crane to build their building, rather than buying, owning, and maintaining the construction crane. Likewise, I.T.'s value proposition for achieving operational effectiveness is akin to "leasing" cloud computing.

The "toolbelt" of I.T. is being at the forefront of innovation, not merely using existing tools and making the use of age old processes, but identifying new and creative solutions that have never been done before that will help its organization do something no one else is doing. It is this innovation in I.T. that brings focus on I.T. as a business enabler than merely as a facilitator of age old processes.

2 UNDERSTANDING THE LEGACY OF I.T. OPERATIONS

Now with Chapter 1 and the vision of the future state of I.T. operations in mind, we'll step back to where many organizations are or recently were, and walk the process through the transition to the modern state. Understanding the legacy model of I.T. Operations is important as an organization can more effectively change and shift to something new if it understands where it currently is and how it got there. As we'll address in this chapter and the rest of this book, the hardest parts in making the transition to the modern state is changing the culture, the thinking, the years of developed and practiced processes of employees to completely new and different daily, weekly, and monthly routines.

Tech as a New Resource in the Marketplace

While civilized societies have been around for hundreds if not thousands of years, "tech" has only been prevalent in the past 40-years. The Internet that has revolutionized most business processes and operations was made available to the general public just two decades ago. The majority of humans have spent more of their lives without the Internet than with the Internet; however in the short period of time, both the young and old now rely on the Internet for their day to day communications, banking, research, and goods procurement.

The smartphone that most everyone has and uses every day to check emails, make phone calls, share photos, and communicate with family, friends, and co-workers was only introduced to the marketplace in the past decade. In a short 10-years, the tool used to find, share, and communicate with others has gone from invention to adoption to day to day usage. Tech is truly a new resource in the marketplace.

Rethinking Entire Business Processes in a Matter of Years

As quickly as tech has been introduced in the marketplace, there has been a complete rethinking of fundamental processes that tech has brought to consumers of information. Retailers have come and gone in the past two decades as the introduction of streaming videos like NetFlix and YouTube have rendered an entire industry of video tapes, DVDs, and movie rental organizations out of existence. Downloadable music and streaming audio services have made CDs and CD-players invented just a decade ago obsolete.

Traditional brick and mortar retailers have had their entire business models change as consumers buy their products over the internet and have goods delivered to them overnight, rather than walking into a store or shopping mall to make purchases. Billions of square feet of retail sales space built over the past decade have to be rethought, redesigned, and remarketed to reflect the new and ever changing behaviors of the modern buyer.

Consumers of goods and services are becoming more knowledgeable and more savvy because they can get expert information at their fingertips by surfing the Internet than going into the store and talking to an expert. Of course, many times the information gathered by an individual on their own by surfing the Internet may not be accurate, but that too is a changing influence and impact on how tech in a few short years is continuing to change the nature of how business is done today as compared with just a few short years ago.

Decision Making Based on an Emerging Market Mentality

The fast paced release of technologies and solutions have evolved so quickly that best practices in utilizing this new information and the new resources has not always kept up with the evolution of products and services. Releases of new solutions has produced several competing solutions, so the selection and adoption of the "right" product or solution has been challenging. Many times technologies have been released that have been adopted in ways that is completely different than what was intended, and that too has impacted what might be the "proper" use of technologies.

The accelerated adoption of technologies has dictated a rushed planning process and resulted in security incidents that have breached confidential information and caused the loss of sensitive information. Specific to cases involving identity theft, misuse of credit card information, and personal data release, once released by breach of security, the information cannot be unbreeched. While a better job could have been done to protect information, it is the nature of fast-paced technology advancements that are moving faster than security practices to protect the information.

And too often, the solution to security breaches hasn't been to slow down and fix faulty processes, rather the solution has been to invent and release newer technologies that just build on top of the older problematic systems. It's like instead of stopping to rethink how to build a building that won't fall over, it's using new technology to merely create a new way to prop up the old building that is leaning over while people are still working or living there.

The emerging market continues to evolve, and it has been the nature of tech to charge forward rather than to step back and plan. As such, moving forward, it is incumbent on to I.T. professionals to not only help shore up the environment as best as possible, but to also minimize risk and challenges caused by technology and improve processes in the ongoing evolution of technological products and services.

Working Hard to Get Early Tech Working

Those who were involved in tech early on have grown up understanding, realizing, and dealing with early tech systems that weren't reliable, prone to failure, and where a model of redundancy and maintenance was needed to keep tech working properly. Anyone in tech for more than ten years has built systems and created backup and redundancy in systems to counter the expected failures of faulty systems. Being in the tech industry supporting early systems meant working long hours, evenings, and weekends keeping systems patched, updated, maintained, and operational.

The belief that "we'll wait for the first update before we deploy anything" came from the early days where products and technologies never worked when they were first released; and organizations just waited until the second generation or update was released before adopting new technology.

Additionally, new technologies didn't always do what they were pitched to do, so a lot of time was spent evaluating systems comparing what they really do vs. what they say they're going to do. "Shoot-outs" comparing one product versus another was commonplace, because with the fast emergence of new technologies, the norm was to plan for something new coming out, doing a side by side comparison, and spending weeks, sometimes months, comparing and evaluating solutions.

The Entire Introduction of Technologies in a Single Lifespan

Because tech has been introduced and adopted in just 20-40 years, the "old timers" in tech have actually lived through the entire lifespan of the evolution of technology that has entered and has changed the marketplace. One good thing about institutional knowledge is having a background of what an organization does, the business cycles in an enterprise, and knowing the management team and the people in a business.

However, the down side of having lived through the entire technological lifecycles of tech in an organization is that as the new cloud-driven environment has evolved, there's now a completely new and different way that enterprises should think about, interact, and leverage the technologies available today. This past experience frequently has led to behaviors and habits built from years of having to build systems based on unreliable hardware, installing software that inherently had bugs and faults, to doing lengthy product to comparisons, habits that need breaking to be able to completely rethink technology adoption today.

When buying a cloud service with an established service level agreement, the organization doesn't need to then buy backup systems for the service as the organization had to do in the days when the environment was built and maintained by the enterprise. Security systems of the past are completely different when large hosted environments spend billions of dollars on security infrastructures compared to the thousands of dollars organizations typically spent on their own.

Bottom-line, while I.T. professionals have spent their entire life seeing how tech has evolved, those with years of knowledge and experience have to rethink the new world of I.T. and reprogram their thinking and perceptions to build a new way of working with tech like never before.

3 CLOUD COMPUTING CHANGING THE FOCUS OF I.T. TO APPLICATIONS AND SERVICES

The need to evolve to a new way of I.T. operations didn't pop up overnight, there has been a steady inclusion of new technologies and services that have created the need for a new operating model. Earlier in the century, the introduction of the "smartphone" provided users a new tool to access their business critical information, causing an initial ripple in the flow of processes within historical I.T. business operations. Next, cloud computing provided early adopter enterprises a glimpse into the new and modern application and data sharing model that drastically simplified applications delivery as a monthly paid service.

Modernizing Applications and Datacenter Operations

Detailed in a previous mini-book series text "Application and Datacenter Modernization" (Morimoto, 2016), the I.T. organizations went through a shift from thinking about "servers and systems" to just providing end users with applications and data through a service. Ultimately this is what users care about, they want to just have access to their information, whether that's email, accounting software, or file access.

Users don't spend time thinking about which version of an operating system their email is hosted on, what version of anti-malware they are running, what the backup and disaster recovery process their system is managed by. Users simply want to send and receive emails, access files, and utilize the data they have created and stored. When applications shifted to service-based models with products like Microsoft Office 365, Box.com, or Salesforce.com, users were provided the end service they've been looking for.

The Rise of Shadow I.T.

In fact, for many organizations, when I.T. didn't provide the basic email, file, or line of business services that users wanted, users simply went online and purchased the cloud service directly from a software provider. This is how many organizations ended up with Box.com for filesharing or Salesforce.com for client relationship management. Users were able to go directly to a software vendor, buy the service and begin using it without I.T.'s involvement.

This direct purchase and delivery of software was completely foreign for I.T. organizations, because for the first time, users were able to provision software without the help of I.T. experts. As a service, users got what they needed, and they were able to fulfill business needs that helped them get their job done.

For many organizations it was a year, two, even three years before I.T. realized how prevalent the direct use of applications were in their organization. Once I.T. realized that users were provisioning and using software outside of the strict processes of I.T. operations, the challenge became securing the data and managing user access to the cloud-based software systems. As many organizations found, without someone monitoring or management, when an employee left the organization, for as long as months later, the former employee still had access to all of the files and data, because no process or procedure was in place to remove the individual's access to the cloud service upon the individual's departure.

In due time, I.T. regained control of these cloud services, converted them into enterprise license agreements, created single sign-on access to the services, and monitored and managed access to these systems. However cloud services entered most enterprises before I.T. was involved, without the need for complex I.T. rules and policies, making enterprises aware that there was an easier way of providing application and data services than was provided in the past.

Leveraging Cloud Computing for Business Application Access

With the introduction of the first Software as a Service (SaaS) cloud hosted offerings, enterprise users and I.T. organizations realized and experienced a simple method of getting access to applications and data.

Rather than in the past where traditional I.T.-led application acquisition required lengthy evaluation, purchase, implementation, and "rollout" processes, SaaS proved that "anyone" could provision software and start using business applications more quickly and without formal I.T. processes.

Introduction of Rolling Updates to Enterprise Applications

As SaaS applications evolved, and new features and functions were rolled into the applications, enterprise users were also introduced to a new servicing model where they get new functionality every few weeks without a major upgrade process pushed out to them every few years. This was a change that had a huge impact on the I.T. industry. Users were willing to accept change to their applications as opposed to traditional thinking that change required structured planning, training, and individual user hand holding.

The rollout of updates was something that was started with the release of updates on mobile phones, where users experienced new updates to their mobile phone operating system and applications every week, and users simply had to tap a key to update their applications without really thinking about it. Users started to get used to the benefit of regular product enhancements rather than having to wait years before something new is finally added to their application for them to get their work done.

This evolution of rolling updates in SaaS applications also minimized the need to buy 3rd party plug-ins to applications when users realized that while an application might lack a certain feature, they just had to wait a few weeks, and new functionality would be added into the application.

The elimination of 3rd party plug-ins has been helpful in the industry in terms of support and upgrade compatibility, as applications can now be updated every few weeks without the concern that some 3rd party add-in stops working because of the update. The vicious cycle of problems and challenges that I.T. has faced for years in managing applications and updates has been simplified by the processes built-in to SaaS-based servicing models.

Selectively Leveraging Cloud Application to Fulfill Business Needs

Some cloud applications perfectly align with the application and data model, whereas some use cases are not fulfilled as effectively with cloud-based solutions (yet). Modernization doesn't mean moving everything to the cloud. There are several use cases where enterprises have continued to host server systems for business applications, albeit some of those servers might be shifted to running as servers in a hosted cloud environment. Not all applications needs to be immediately moved to cloud based SaaS offerings.

As an example, many organizations with highly sensitive patient health records, content with government defense data, or highly protected trade secret information may have restrictions on how or where the data is stored. Usually, cloud is no less secure than other methods that organizations have used in the past, but it's more related to experience that executives and security professionals have, legal contract limitations, or other factors that limit what organizations feel comfortable storing in cloud services. In these cases, traditional on-premise systems are perfectly fine for organizations to continue to use.

For most enterprises, some data is stored as cloud services, while other applications and data run on traditional server systems. As organizations offload part of their enterprise I.T. systems to cloud-based services, that percentage of systems offloads I.T. from having to manage those systems. In time, organizations find that 20%, 40%, 70% of their systems are running as cloud-systems. This drastically decreases the traditional workload that I.T. has to manage and shifts the way I.T. needs to provides services in the future.

Changing Business Operations in the Era of Cloud Computing

As applications move to new operational states like SaaS, I.T. organizations have to shift how they monitor, manage, administer, and support the applications and user's interactions with the applications. Rather than traditional software deployment mechanisms used in the past, cloud-based applications using Web browsers or mobile phone apps require a different mechanism to manage and update the "client software" used by users every day.

Additionally, as SaaS-based applications have no servers, databases, web servers, system patching, or server updating as traditional applications, I.T. organizations no longer have to do the day to day management of the infrastructure for the application(s) as has been the process for years. There are still key components that I.T. needs to manage such as monitoring the service that the SaaS application is running, so if the SaaS service provider is "down," that I.T. is aware of the provider outage and can inform users, and potentially get on the phone and get updates as to when the service will be back up and running.

Also, as SaaS applications run over the Internet, I.T. operations have to ensure the connectivity to the Internet is stable and reliable. The movement to SaaS applications creates different areas that I.T. has to oversee and manage, something that has been covered in another mini-book series book titled "Adapting to the New World of I.T." (Morimoto, 2017). In the

Adapting to the New World of I.T. book, the change in focus of application services and management still exists, but the day to day tasks for I.T. operations change.

For many organizations, as the business shifts from a traditional on-premise state to a cloud-hosted model, I.T. finds that it is doing double duty, as there are still applications, servers, and systems running on-premise, while the organization adds new applications and services as cloud-based services. Until the organization eliminates the traditional on-premise component, I.T. models won't fully change. This is why it behooves an organization to rapidly make the transition to modern systems than to straddle both traditional and modern systems. Until then, I.T. will be burdened with double the work rather than achieving simplification of operations.

CLOUD COMPUTING CHANGING THE FOCUS OF I.T. TO APPLICATIONS AND SERVICES

4 CLOUD-BASED APPLICATIONS AND SERVICES AS A TRANSITION STATE

I.T. management and operations typically still think about and look to implementing legacy practices versus adapting new and modern systems and processes. Even though cloud-based applications and services can be leveraged to do much more, because of years of historical experiences for how to design, architect, manage, and support I.T. systems, many times I.T. personnel decisions do not represent forward thinking. This chapter clarifies the transition state for I.T. operations as organizations shift from systems and processes of the past, into newer, more applicable models of the future.

Transitioning I.T. Operations to a Cloud Computing Model

Initial implementations of SaaS and cloud computing models place I.T. operations in a transitional state, with new solutions being provided as a service in a cloud model, while the organization still has years of investments, processes, and operations based on an on-premise based model. Unless an organization completely shifts an application over to a cloud model in an expedited manner, the organization remains with a hybrid configuration that requires traditional support services in addition to new model for services.

During the transition process, organizations that have large enterprise monitoring, patching, security controls, and management systems can't simply cut the management systems in half just because half the applications have been moved to the cloud. Many times the management systems have distributed server systems, databases, and configurations that have been built-up and scaled to support the entire enterprise environment and cannot be easily pared back.

As such, the transition period as organizations shift to a cloud computing model doesn't necessarily seem to decrease the overall footprint of the enterprise's I.T. operations. However that doesn't mean that some changes and modernization can't be made, it just requires the timing and scope of the downsizing of I.T. operational systems during the transition period need to be assessed, especially if the transition period is anticipated to take a year or more. If the organization will be in a transition state long term, then parallel efforts should be made to decrease the footprint of the operations systems while on-premise servers and systems are eliminated from active operations.

On-premise Administration and Managements Models Inefficient for Cloud-based Applications

On-premise systems require a significant amount of care and feeding that includes monitoring, hardware maintenance, "watching blinking lights of systems", temperature/cooling, electronical power management, system redundancy, site replication, operating platform and application patching/updating. SaaS applications have no need for many of these services, so the parts of I.T. operations that provide these services to the organization need to rethink what services are needed, and rethink their future role in the organization.

As an example, as email servers were transitioned to cloud-based SaaS applications like Microsoft's Office 365, the number of systems and processes needed to manage the on-premise environment were drastically reduced. Organizations no longer needed the hardware that hosted the email servers and the multiple replicas of email databases in both their primary site as well as in remote sites and replicas stored in disaster recovery sites. Eliminating email on-premise meant eliminating anti-spam filter servers, anti-virus systems, tape or storage backup that was used to backup terabytes and terabytes of emails, and the monitoring systems that were used to track the operations of the email system.

Granted, some of these services are still needed such as backup and monitoring systems to manage other systems other than email. However, many organizations have found that with the elimination of email and nightly backups of the email system, that the backup system was able to be drastically pared down.

Additionally, the personnel needed to manage the systems moved to the cloud needs to be changed as well. For organizations that had teams of individuals managing and maintaining email systems, the number of support personnel also needs to be evaluated for paring back, with individuals reassigned to other tasks in the enterprise. Just because the organization no longer has to monitor and manage its own email system doesn't mean that I.T. operations cease to function. There are many tasks within enterprises that require ongoing services, and individuals can be shifted to new roles as applicable.

Applying Archaic Management Models to Modern Application Systems

Too often, rather than rethinking about new models of I.T. operations, we see organizations trying to shoehorn legacy ways of managing and maintaining systems to modern application and data hosted systems. Newer application service models require new methods of monitoring and managing the systems.

As an example, some I.T. professionals want to set up backup systems, so they can back up their SaaS-based applications like Microsoft Office 365 emails and files. This thinking focused on what happens if the Office 365 email content gets corrupt or what happens if ransomware attacks the organization and encrypts the SharePoint Online and OneDrive cloud files? In the past, the best practice has been to have a tape backup to restore content in those circumstances.

Backups however are not needed in backing up reliable and reputable vendor cloud-stored solutions. Mailbox corruption and ransomware type attacks have not been a challenge for cloud services solutions like Microsoft's Office 365.

Microsoft's Office 365 mailboxes are stored very differently and managed in a way that mailbox corruption (and thus the need to restore mailboxes for corruption purposes) has not been an issue in the 7+ years that Microsoft has been running Office 365. Mailbox corruptions occurred in early day Microsoft Exchange (on-premise) due to the nature of 32-bit operating systems and simple ESE database technology used in early versions of Exchange. With significant updates to Exchange 2013 and now in Exchange 2016, Microsoft uses exclusively a 64-bit platform that doesn't limit mailbox size and indexing, and thus mailbox corruption that organizations experienced years ago doesn't occur in current releases of

Exchange and Office 365. The latest release of Office 365 has a background worker thread that runs continuously to manage database inconsistencies so that problems from the past are no longer experienced. It is the cloud vendor's responsibility to maintain the integrity of the data and messages, and it has yet to be seen or experienced by ANY CCO customers using Office 365.

As for Ransomware attacks, to date, the Ransomware attacks have been caused by filesystem level exploits of old/archaic transport level communications, or more simply stated, older filesystems used on-premise that allowed Ransomware encryption of files. Files stored in Office 365 do not use the older filesystem protocols that have been the target of ALL ransomware attack vectors used in the past. If an organization using SharePoint Online or OneDrive for Business were compromised with any of the previously released Ransomware malware, the content in Office 365 would not be affected.

That said, new malware vectors could be released that could potentially impact Office 365 filesystems. A couple solutions around that.

- Use of Microsoft's E5 "Advanced Threat Detection Security" that intercepts ALL emails and attachments, scans the content for invalid (and potentially threatening code) and quarantines all content. This is commonly called "anti-ransomware" technologies. It goes beyond anti-malware technologies (formerly known as anti-virus software) that requires a virus to be identified for a filter to be implemented in the anti-malware software. Anti-ransomware technology is not dependent on previous attacks, and addresses "zero-day" attacks by looking at the behavior of emails / attachments, and blocking malicious looking content before users get the content. This feature comes in Microsoft's E5 licensing and can (should) be enabled for any enterprise looking to stay 1 step ahead of the "bad guys"
- Microsoft also has an additional component that provides advanced threat detection security in their "CloudApp" platform that extends anti-ransomware beyond emails and attachments to ALL content uploaded/downloaded to Office 365 through the enterprise's firewalls/proxy. CloudApp provides perimeter level protections for the scanning and protection of content. This is a secondary defense that prevents malicious content from entering the enterprise.

When all else fails, SharePoint Online / OneDrive has the ability to store "revisions" of content. If ransomware makes its way into the enterprise and somehow injects itself into the SharePoint / OneDrive Online infrastructure, with revisioning enabled, any N-level revisions that are infected / encrypted can be deleted and replaced by N-1 revisions (i.e., the previous revision of content) that existed before the ransomware attack.

Again, these scenarios have not been experienced in the past, however there are several built-in solutions that Microsoft provides to minimize, present, and even recover (if needed) assuming the appropriate licenses have been purchased, enabled, and managed.

The Need to Backup Cloud-based Data

The question still comes back, should an organization backup their cloud-based data? The common answer is that the organization "could" choose to back up their cloud-based data, but if runs I.T. the way that the tools and technologies exist TODAY, then there are better and smarter ways of doing things.

Organizations have traditionally backed up stuff because I.T. of the past did a poor job handling security and frequently had old outdated systems in place that allowed ransomware to sneak in. If I.T. was optimally managed (even 5-10 years ago), most organizations would have been able to avoid corrupt mailboxes and ransomware attacks. In the modern era of computing, the technologies exist and best practices are followed in cloud-provider environments, better than what most organizations could afford to do in traditional on-premise datacenter environments.

A common point of information used to bring clarity into the value of backing up digital data is thinking back just a decade or two ago. In the "paper days", organizations had legal contracts and documents. They'd put those important documents in fire proof safes and/or shipped them to an offsite file storage facility (like DataSafe or Iron Mountain). The documents were never photocopied 2 or 3 times and stored in 2 or 3 different locations. While a building could be knocked down because of an earthquake or flooded by a hurricane, organizations didn't buy and build in overly redundant systems. If the organization didn't (nor does) photocopy every bit of printed information and store it in 2 or 3 different locations, why do that with the digital data?

Usually the reason organizations are more protective about their digital data is because I.T. personnel grew up in an era where computer hardware was prone to failure ("crash"), where patches and updates caused systems to fail. It was a necessity to have a backup to recover from what effectively was a faulty legacy infrastructure.

In the new world of thinking, emails and files stored in Microsoft's Office 365 are already replicated across three separate Office 365 datacenters in a region. All content that is deleted remains in a recovery or recycle bin for restoral. Organizations can place their content on Litigation Hold that then retains a copy of ALL content created, modified, deleted, or even overwritten where administrators can recover corrupt content.

Backup would not be the second line of defense for cloud-stored content, a backup would actually be about 6 or 7 levels deep as a cloud-hosted provider like Microsoft is already providing high availability, disaster recovery, versioning, along with a number of layers of security, anti-ransomware, controlled folder access, and the like.

Good analogies for this are you don't buy a car to have a spare backup for your Rental Car or you don't have a spare house in the same neighborhood that you live in just in case your house burns down or is damaged in an earthquake. Therefore, why have a spare email or file storage system to back up a cloud service like Office 365 that has a Service Level Agreement that is better than organizations have had on their own for years…

It is a whole new model for business services, and one that requires completely new thinking on the value or need for traditional I.T. management functions like a backup.

The Need to Modernize I.T. Operations

When organizations are in the transition process to the cloud and only have one or two cloud-based applications, the organization maintaining a hybrid load of traditional management systems and modern management systems might be necessary.

However once an organizations shifts past 30%, 40%, or 50% of its applications being in a SaaS or cloud model, then I.T. needs to enact plans to start paring down legacy management systems and rethinking management of modern models, not with existing tools, but using solutions that are most appropriate for a cloud-based environment.

Paring down existing systems means that if an organization had 8 systems running management infrastructure and now the organization has half of its business application systems migrated to the cloud, can the organization eliminated half of the management systems and pare that down to scale. And as new applications have been added to the cloud, are the monitoring, management, and security systems used over the past decade still applicable to the new cloud-based applications? Even if the existing tool has a plug-in or module for cloud management, are there better tools, services, and solutions available to maintain, manage, and support a cloud-hosted business model.

These changes extend beyond just rolling existing systems into modern models, but a rethinking of I.T. operations as it relates to performing day to day tasks, managing systems, and supporting the organization in a completely new manner to meet the new business needs of the organization.

5 RETHINKING I.T. SECURITY AND I.T. OPERATIONS

For organization that are serious about network security, those organizations are almost certainly implementing networking and security in their environments based on age-old proven best practices. Unfortunately, those best practices are exactly the reason that ALL of the biggest security attacks (like Equifax, WannaCry, Anthem Health, Home Depot) and the thousands that haven't made front page news have occurred. The "bad guys" are well aware of the security best practice playbook and know it's not worth their time to go attack all of the overly hardened and protected systems and configurations enterprises have implemented. All of the big network breaches didn't occur because someone found a way to break down the "front door". In every case, the network was compromised through a weak link in the enterprise. This chapter covers the model of rethinking I.T. security and I.T. operations more applicable to the current modern environment.

Exploits Through the Side Door, not the Front Door

In the case of WannaCry, the exploit was a hole in the Windows 7 operating system patched years ago. In the case of Equifax, the exploit compromised a well-known database bug that the attackers targeted. In the case of Anthem Health, it was a phishing attack that opened a clear remote path into the enterprises datacenter. For the breach of Target Stores, the attack was traced back to a compromise of an external vendor that laid open a pathway into Target's enterprise.

For each of these enterprises with networking professionals in network operation centers (NOCs) monitoring millions of dollars in security systems, all of these exploits triggered NO alarms, NO warnings. Why?

The simple answer is the "bad guys" have the network implementation playbook and know what triggers warnings, so sensors are implemented to work around the well documented security systems. It's like every spy or heist movie you've watched, where the bad guys know where the guards stand, what time they take breaks, and which security cameras have "blind spots" that of course the "bad guys" know of and use to their advantage.

The Logical Solution to the Security Problem

Every enterprise relying on the same "best security appliance" utilizing the same "industry best practice" doing the same thing company to company that has "always worked" needs to modernize their security strategies and practices! Said in another way, if you're doing everything the way everyone else is doing it, based on well documented best practices, the way "you've always done it," you MUST change!

Your organization has to change its I.T. playbook. You have to get rid of all of the (common) weak links in the enterprise. In most cases the change isn't just technology, but will take a refocus on people, policy and processes that will shake up an enterprise, but if security is important for your organization and you want to prevent your enterprise from ending up being the next company on the front page news for a security attack, change must happen!

What Change is Necessary?

The common factors for all security breaches comes down to people, convenience, and interruption. For the past couple decades, I.T. has treated users with kid gloves, we don't want to interrupt or inconvenience users. If a user is using a (really old) utility or version of software that they "like" and are unable or unwilling to learn something new, that utility, program, or their entire operating environment is left in a downgraded state to support the user. Or, if an urgent update becomes available, rather than applying the update immediately as we should, we wait until it is convenient for the users before the update is applied. Or, when it's time to upgrade systems, we spend months testing software application compatibility, do user training, and babysit users through the upgrade process (sometimes extending an upgrade 6, 12, 24 months) to ensure everyone is handheld through the process.

Why is Time of Essence?

Security breaches caused by outdated software are preventable. While most high profile breaches have software bugs identified months and even years before the security breach occurred, the timeline of security breaches occurring closer to the time the flaw is identified is decreasing. Zero-day attacks are becoming more of a reality, and enterprises need to ready their environments to apply updates within days instead of within weeks/months that is common for many organizations.

Latest Version versus Latest Patches

Many enterprises take false comfort believing that because they have the latest patches applied on a 10-year old version of software that they are fine. However compared to having the latest version of software (that is fully patched and updated), old software is old software. Those running Windows 7 in the era of 3rd generation Windows 10 are running a version of Windows that was written shortly after the first smartphones were released to the general public! Granted, your Windows 7 might be fully patched and updated covering all known bugs, but the technological innovation or more so the security innovation in the past decade are significant. What software developers have learned in the past decade and have included in the new version of Windows 10 compared to Windows 7 is significant.

In a recent hackathon test running Windows 10 that was released in the Fall of 2017 compared to a fully patched release of Windows 7 that was released in 2009, many of the hacking utilities used in the tests couldn't even be copied onto an out of the box configuration of Windows 10. With Windows Defender enabled by default on the Windows 10 systems, the utilities were immediately disabled and quarantined; whereas Windows 7 had no built-in technology of that type and allowed the copying and storage of tools.

On Windows 7, users were typically also local administrators that had full access to the local operating system; whereas with Windows 10, while a user could be made a local administrator, current best practices profile role-based security on Windows 10 systems, and administrative controls are granted to administrators on a temporary access basis only when certain functions are run. Thus, by default, a Windows 10 system had no native administrator role running on the system to easily compromise.

The Value (or Lack of Value) of an Age-old Network Penetration Test - Network Penetration Tests or Pen Tests are common practices for enterprises checking their security. However using the "front door" vs "side door" security analogy, the Pen Test checks the front door for security, which most enterprises have hardened their firewalls, locked down ports, and run intrusion detection systems (IDS) to monitor edge security. However, the "bad guys" know the edge is protected, just like the common thief knows not to try to break down the front door of a house or building in plain sight, but instead simply goes to the side or back of the home or building, and frequently finds a door propped open, an unlocked window, or follow someone in as they exit.

Pen Tests are important as the front door most certainly needs to be locked down and secured, but unfortunately they provide organizations a false sense of security because a strong-arm breach of the perimeter isn't how security breaches occur.

Security is Only as Strong as the Weakest Link

This is where all of this comes together. Enterprise security isn't merely having old products patched and updated. And security isn't merely ensuring the network perimeter passes a penetration test. In security breaches, it is the weakest link that is compromised that creates an open door into the enterprise datacenter. It is gaining access by walking right through the front door of a network through a valid VPN connection from a compromised Windows 7 endpoint; or gaining access by phishing the credentials of an administrator that has way too much privileged access to remotely access sensitive information from compromised credentials; or malware injected in an email that slipped into the organization like any other email, but a user opening the message containing ransomware compromises the integrity of the network.

What Can be Done to Improve Network Security?

Taking all of the above into account, if security protection is important for the organization, then updating to the latest version of software and keeping that software patched and updated is the best thing to do. That means getting rid of older versions of operating systems, software programs, and utilities and starting to use the latest versions of software even if that means inconveniencing users and forcing them to learn something new. It's what the National Transportation Safety Board (NTSB) forced the airline industry to do, accept delays, accept the inconvenience to passengers to fix problems or potential problems, so that planes don't crash and kill people.

In tech, it's keeping the latest versions of software up to date, replacing old systems not just patching them together forever. It means installing rolling updates, even if that means inconveniencing users and occasionally causing an unexpected outage all for the purpose of preventing an even more debilitating major security breach or being forced to shut down because of a ransomware attack on key systems.

This is a completely new mindset for enterprises. This will take a bit of relearning the experience of users versus the risk caused by having older systems even if they are fully patched and updated. No longer will it be acceptable to have 10-year old, even 5-year old software and systems in the enterprise. This also bodes well for the argument that cloud services are better than internal datacenter services because for organizations that amortize equipment over 3-5 years and try to stretch usage to 5-7 years have to consider the benefit of leveraging cloud services that constantly update their offerings every 6-12 months in rolling updates.

How to Minimize Interruption to Critical Business Applications in the New World of Thinking?

Upgrading and updating systems to the latest version of software or updates can be disruptive to the ongoing usage and operation of an application. However an organization can minimize the impact caused by patches and updates by taking advantage of the latest technologies like rolling cluster updates (on backend server systems) and minimizing the number of old/unique "plug-ins" on client systems. For technologies built in to Windows Server 2016 as an example, an organization can have a cluster that is upgraded node by node, while the cluster maintains operational. The nodes of the cluster are patched, updated, and rebooted as necessary and with regular frequency without bringing the cluster down or having to stop application services.

For databases like SQL Server 2016 and 2017, leveraging new features such as Always On Availability Group technology, Servers can be updated node by node without bringing SQL Services offline.

For endpoint devices like Windows, Macs, iPhones, Android Phones, and tablets, the use of "modern apps" that effectively "float" on top of the operating system allows for better experiences when the operating system is patched, updated, or upgraded. The use of fewer "3rd party add-ins" and the added features embedded in core applications minimizes the upgrade and integration challenges as software and systems are upgraded and updated on a rolling basis.

These are integrated technologies built in to the latest versions of software that didn't exist just 5-years ago. So while an organization may seek to implement the latest patches and updates on 5 - 10 year old software, there is a disruption caused by system reboots, driver changes, and things that were part of older technologies that no longer exist in modern applications. Again, technological improvements added into the latest release of software that thinks ahead to the need for enterprises to patch, update, and reboot systems, but in a manner that can be done with NO interruption of services of the application state in use.

What About Highly Regulated Systems that Can't be Upgraded so Frequently?

For highly regulated systems that cannot be upgraded so frequently, an organization needs to consider placing those systems in a "closed environment", effectively isolating the systems "off the net" with NO remote access or remote connectivity even to other internal systems (that may be connected to the Internet). Having fully isolated environments can minimize the risk of the older, higher security risk systems from being compromised when the ONLY way to access those systems is from a dedicated hardwired connection directly to the systems.

Back to the Inconvenience Factor

Many administrators may complain that having systems that require physical connections from limited number of systems will be inconvenient to manage. However, that is the solution to one of the problems with network administration these days, who want to be able to administer, manage, monitor, and maintain systems from "anywhere", from the convenience of their home, home office, or phone. It's that convenience that creates a whole line of risk as the systems, when made accessible for management and administration, also opens up the door for remote breach of security.

6 ACCEPTING THE NEW MODEL OF OPERATING SYSTEMS AND APPLICATIONS AS SERVICES

The "as a service" model is at the core of most organizations' applications and operating environments. And in order for I.T. operations to shift their role and services to meet the needs of the current and future model of operations, I.T. needs to accept this new model of applications and operating systems as services. This is easier said than done as I.T. personnel have spent the better part of two decades perfecting the monolithic models that have been foundational in I.T. operations. To walk away from years of conditioning leaves I.T. personnel uncomfortable as the core processes of maintaining systems are disregarded. However it is key for personnel to "let go" and move on to the new model of operations.

Assessing the Enterprises Shift to Modern Solutions and Services

As noted earlier in this book, when organizations first implement modern (cloud/SaaS-based) solutions, their management and operations strategies for technologies tend to remain as they have been. However as an organization reaches 30, 40, 50% of its critical business applications having been modernized, the organization needs to start to shift to modern management solutions and services as well. It starts off with an assessment for where the organization stands. In quantifying, it's typically looking at the percentage of the top 10-12 applications that the organization leverages daily (email, file sharing, telephony, accounting, point of sales, manufacturing controls) not the hundreds of smaller utilities and tools, and not I.T. specific administration and management tools, just the key business user-focused applications. When that hits 30-40% modernized, the organization needs to be shifting I.T. operations to modern models as well.

Understanding Modern Methods of Monitoring Modern Applications (monitoring service (user access), not servers/systems, monitoring functional states (send/receive)

Shifting Modern Administration to Meet the Needs of Cloud-based Application Models

Administration is relegated to just adding/deleting users, setting up permissions/access, enabling features/functions. Key difference is cloud-based apps frequently release new updates every 2-4 weeks, so it's about being on top of the new feature releases and behaviors and managing new functionality (making sure the organization knows what features are added, and how organizations can leverage them). There's no immediately blocking everything new, as new feature rollouts are a good thing for users, I.T. just needs to be aware of the new features and educate itself on how the features work. Monitoring default behaviors (things that used to be disabled by default many times) are enabled by default.

Leveraging Early Fast, Early Slow, and Other New Release Options

Most cloud-based applications provide access to release models, sometimes called "rings", where some users in an organization can be set on a fast ring for new feature release, others on a slow ring for new feature release, many times providing 2 or 3 early release profiles to allow early access experiences of cloud platforms. The new model is setting active users to be participants in the early release model to understand new features/updates, validate usability, and prepare the enterprise in its leveraging of new features and functions.

Rethinking New Feature Enablement, Not Old Function Compatibility

There's a big shift from seeing early adopter testing rings now as tools to finding compatibility issues and blocking the release of new features. Key is to accept that the new features are being rolled out and are the new/ongoing standard and to develop ways to embrace the change, not block it. If an older application is incompatible with a pending new feature release, rather than stopping the advancement of the new feature rollout, spending time looking at the older application that is creating the issue and seeing if that application can be brought forward into a new or modern application. Knowing what is new in applications frequently enables organizations to consolidate products. So, instead of having 10 apps that all have to work together, consolidating to three apps that are all better integrated and moving forward, rather than holding back.

ACCEPTING THE NEW MODEL OF OPERATING SYSTEMS AND APPLICATIONS AS SERVICES

7 DEVELOPING SPLIT MODELS FOR APPLICATIONS AND SERVICES

In the transition state as enterprises shift from on-premise datacenter models to modern cloud and optimized application and data utilizing models, there are two or potentially more disparate systems to manage and maintain. I.T. no longer runs a one size fits all model for applications and systems management. For the 80-90% of commodity applications services that are run and handled "as services", I.T. just needs to "let go" and let the SaaS provider handle security, redundancy, and controls. For the remaining 10-20% core business applications, I.T. can focus on these applications whether as managing them as Platform as a Service model applications, hosted applications, or potentially remaining on-premise. The split model for applications and services becomes the norm for enterprises moving toward the model of optimized application and data services.

Accepting Dual or Multi-Method Administration and Management

Counter to the efforts of I.T. over the past decade of unifying complex I.T. management systems to a common method and process with applications in multiple environments, a split model of management and

DEVELOPING SPLIT MODELS FOR APPLICATIONS AND SERVICES

administration is necessary. What I.T. needs to do is break down its normal day to day tasks and identify which tasks are no longer needed in models where applications or platforms are run as services versus legacy applications that are still running on-premise with hardware to monitor and manage.

The typical tasks IT conducts in daily operations:

- Hardware Maintenance and Management: With on-premise systems, organizations had hardware (servers, racks, switches, appliances) to install, upgrade, maintain, cool, replace, and update). Applications moved to a cloud-based model, whether as a SaaS or PaaS model no longer have any hardware component that I.T. has to deal with. This typically eliminates the need to do much of the physical environment monitoring, environmental control and site disaster recovery work performed by I.T.

- Internal Networking: Network switches and communication systems between servers and systems tied the various hardware pieces together. However with SaaS and PaaS based models, there is no longer a need to interconnect server systems together. All of the switching, routing, dual path, and connectivity is no longer applicable in cloud-based models

- External Networking: Connectivity from a site to the cloud provider, whether a direct connection or communications over the Internet, is still required. However, organizations really need to rethink the architecture for connecting users to cloud systems. Where organizations have created complex and expensive networking systems to connect users to various on-premise and site to site systems, the model can be redone to now more properly reroute users simply to a couple (or even a handful) of cloud providers.

- Storage Systems: For the past decade, storage systems have been built and expanded to handle the exponential growth of storage of files, emails, and system images. However as workloads are moved to the cloud with terabytes of data moved as well, the need for storage systems, storage backup system, replicated and redundant storage systems can be eliminated. Organizations need to rapidly identify what information has been moved and complete the process of wiping storage devices and backup systems of data that has been deemed moved and managed elsewhere.

- Virtualization Hosts: Along with storage, organizations have virtualization hosts and the management systems that go along with it to manage hundreds if not thousands of virtual machines. These systems start to become unnecessary as systems are moved to the cloud. Virtual Machines that once provided server system operations along with all of the associated replicas in remove sites, test and dev systems, and backups of image systems, need to be removed and eliminated.

- Patching and Updating Systems: With a legacy of physical and virtual systems, organizations have patching and updating systems that were built up to maintain the operation of images on systems. While there may still be the need to patch and update remaining on-premise systems; when 40,%, 60%, 80% of an organization's environment has been moved to the cloud, the management systems that supported that model is no longer needed in the size, scope, or volume it once was.
- Monitoring Systems: With significantly fewer applications and server systems inhouse, an organization needs to clean up the monitoring and security systems that oversaw the systems in operations. Again, an organization may not be able to eliminate everything; however, most certainly the organization can cut back the number of monitoring systems commensurate with the number of application systems the organization has eliminated from its management.

As the organization eliminates dozens of systems that ran, monitored, and managed the legacy environment, the organization can consolidate systems to minimize its I.T. operational footprint. If the organization doesn't clean up its existing environment or if it continues to run in a hybrid model, the ability for the organization to truly take advantage of cloud benefits will be prolonged as the organization runs existing legacy systems and adds in workloads to manage the new cloud-based systems.

Dual Model for Administration and Management Does Mean More Complexity

For the short period of time where legacy systems still exist in the environment, yet new systems are brought online, the organization will have a more complex environment. This is that period noted where there will be dual models for administration and management as new systems will be managed differently than legacy systems.

What is important to note is that the reference to this dual model means to rethink the administration and management systems in use and not necessarily reusing the existing systems to monitor and manage the new cloud-based environments. Many times, the administration and management systems will have "support" to manage and maintain new cloud based systems; however in reality, all the legacy management system vendor did was put in basic support to manage the modern systems. The legacy management system itself may need to be completely overhauled and replaced with a modern management system more appropriate and applicable to the new model of modern computing.

Modern Systems Requiring More Simplified Models of Management

Modern systems management requires a much simpler model for management. Instead of a monitoring system that has "nodes" in multiple datacenters monitoring hardware, power, temperature, storage systems, virtual network systems, applications and the like, a system that monitors and manages SaaS and PaaS systems is merely monitoring the operational state of applications.

"As a Service" monitoring is validating that users have access to the service, that effectively the service is "up". And in many cases, the SaaS and PaaS service has monitoring and notification systems that can be configured to alert an organization of a known failure or outage. So, rather than setting up a system to monitor the service, a notification can be enabled by the service provider to send a notice or alert.

The simpler I.T. can make the monitoring and management of modern systems, the less I.T. needs to run and manage complex management systems to oversee simple cloud-based services.

Embracing Management as a Service Model for I.T. Operations

Just as applications have shifted to an "as a service model", I.T. operations can be shifted to an "as a service model". These simpler monitoring and management systems for cloud-based services do not need to be on-premise monolithic systems. Cloud-services for monitoring, incident management, alerting, and all-up dashboard views can be purchased as services as well.

As organizations shift away from on-premise physical and virtual systems, an inventory of remaining systems can help the organization understand what remains in terms of actual operating production systems. For many organizations, even months or years after moving applications and data to the cloud, they determine many of the systems are still running, being backed up, and being maintained in the environment.

The modern I.T. Operations model needs to inventory the environment and determine what can be eliminated and how many systems remain that are legacy management systems themselves. For organizations that eliminate production application systems, with just 20% to 40% of systems remaining on-premise, the organization shouldn't have dozens of management systems remaining.

When the organization is about 50% applications in the cloud, the new management as a service model needs to be embraced to enable the organization to shift away from a heavy load of systems on-premise to monitor and manage systems that now reside in the cloud.

More Modern Applications, Minimization of I.T. Time for Mundane Tasks

With 50% or 80% of business applications running modern applications that require just 20-30% of the time needed for administration, I.T. teams have more time to do other things. Just like with robotics and automation systems, the mundane tasks of monitoring power, temperature, and blinking lights of systems has been eliminated from I.T.'s realm of daily management. Moving to a SaaS and PaaS based model means the elimination of the role of running around unboxing hardware, installing systems, and maintaining those systems.

Additionally, the tasks of "spinning up hosts" or "building virtual machines" has been eliminated too. Much of I.T.'s time over the past half-decade has been spent building test, dev, and production systems along with all of the tasks of maintaining those systems. When an acquisition of another company means adding 300 users to the environment in 30-days, adding those users to a cloud-based email system, a cloud-based file sharing system, a cloud-based telephony system, and adding some of the users to accounting and line of business systems is merely just running a script to insert names to the organization's directory and enabling cloud-based services for user access to applications.

The organization no longer has to spend weeks building hardware capacity and adding systems to accommodate the growth of the organization. Likewise, as users move between sites or business units, the shift in a cloud-based application model typically means a single user profile edit will reflect a change in roles and permissions. Data doesn't need to be moved between organizational servers and sites. Even in a divestiture where hundreds of users are moved to a completely different company, in cloud-based systems, a new tenant is created and mailboxes and file folders are simply migrated from one cloud tenant to another.

No hardware needs to be setup, configured, moved, or managed. What used to take weeks to prep a datacenter for the startup of a new business unit or organization now can be done in a matter of days by simply spinning up new services and moving data. Processes can be changed and drastically simplified with modern applications and application management.

Reshaping I.T. to Focus on Effective Business Services

I.T.'s new day to day role is to now focus on setting new Service Level Agreements and setting expectations on outcomes of differing I.T. services between Legacy vs Modern. Critical business roles emerge from an I.T. department no longer burdened with mundane daily tasks. I.T. can now focus more on the business, what their organization actually does to generate revenue and service its constituents.

For many I.T. organizations, it's spending time going out into the business operations, whether that's visiting retail storefronts, seeing how the organization's products are manufactured and sold, meeting with doctors and patients, seeing how financial transactions are handled, working side by side sales and field personnel. It's spending time with users throughout the enterprise to truly understand what the business does and how business is currently conducted.

Knowing what is done day to day in the organization helps I.T. get a vision of the routines and processes of the organization, and with a little creative understanding of technology and technology services, I.T. can rethink how technology can benefit the end users of the organization.

I.T. personnel become more like business analysts, personnel that understand the tasks and routines of people and processes in the organization. By understanding the business, and knowing current technologies like data analytics, cognitive services, and Internet of Things, I.T. organizations can build new services to help employees in the organization do things easiest, better, and more effectively.

8 BUSINESS SERVICES FOCUSED ON REVENUE GENERATING ACTIVITIES

In describing the future model of business services that I.T. operations shifts to post datacenter transitions to modern "as a service" models, this chapter provides case scenarios that helps to frame and create visualization of what I.T. personnel are doing that are direct revenue generating activities.

Case Scenario – Redistributing Inventory Based on Projected Needs

One scenario where I.T. has been successful driving top-line growth is helping organizations that sell goods and services identify areas of need and shifting products and resources to those locations. For one retailer that sells products across hundreds of locations in a country, in traditional models, products would be distributed equally to all stores coast to coast. However once an inventory and sales monitoring system was put in place, the organization found that certain products sold better in some stores than others; and during different times of year, certain products would sell even better in some stores than others.

By reviewing the sales and trends, the I.T. organization was able to determine that certain products such as umbrellas, raincoats, boots, plastic sheeting, and paper products sold better in stores where there were rainstorms and foul weather. By monitoring weather forecasts 7-10 days in advance and then moving inventory of these goods to stores that are projected to get foul weather, by placing these goods in strategic places that made it easy for customers to come in and buy these goods, the organization was able to increase sales in those stores by 18%-32%. Over an initial 6-month period of monitoring, those stores no longer ran out of key foul weather goods, whereas stores without foul weather had no need for those goods. Thus, the rebalance of inventory drastically improved overall business revenues.

Taken one step further, the organization that tracked what other goods were commonly purchased during foul weather, determined that people bought chocolate products as well as junk food items (chips, cookies, instant noodles); so the placement of those items near the foul weather umbrellas and plastic goods resulted in an uptick in purchases of these items in those stores by 9%.

A simple analysis of purchase history as it relates to weather conditions helped an organization rebalance its inventory and increase revenues without having to increase advertising expenditures or finding additional sources of revenue.

Case Scenario – Providing Necessary Resources In Times of Emergency Needs

In a similar scenario to foul weather projections relating to product sales and inventory redistribution, an organization with retail stores selling home and garden goods found that its ability to rebalance inventory of key goods to areas with forecasts for hurricanes drastically improved the organization's ability to better support its customers in times of emergencies.

The organization moved goods typically purchased during hurricane warnings like plywood, batteries, electric generators, bricks, sand, burlap sacks, and water. While it seems to be common sense, traditional models that balance inventory across a region may show a high volume of goods in a region; however consumers don't buy goods throughout a region, when weather forecasts target more specific communities, that's when specific stores are hit with immediate requests for goods.

By simply tying the inventory management system to do predictive analysis on weather patterns far away, an organization can start moving certain goods to a region, and then to stores in specific communities.

This helped the organization fulfill on the needs of its customers, balance stock to those who needed it, anticipated needs so that shelves could be restocked in advance of a disaster rather than trying to move goods after an event has occurred and roadways were closed.

Case Scenario – Shifting from Blanket Marketing Campaigns to Targeted Sales Campaigns

Organizations have used targeted advertising campaigns for years sending mailers to specific zip codes of neighborhoods more likely to buy their goods and services. However in an era where data on consumer spending can target even tighter demographic controls, leveraging this information can make targeted campaigns of just a decade ago seem like blanket marketing.

As an example, rather than advertising to an entire zip code in hope that "someone" in that area is interested in a product or service, just as users have found online retailers use very specific target marketing, a user specifically searching for Size 0 baby diapers is likely expecting a newborn. That buyer is also a good target to purchase baby wipes, a diaper pail, a baby car seat, crib, and infant clothing.

Data is more readily available than ever before, and when used properly, information can be used to help, not only to sell goods and services to someone who might need it, but to utilize predictive analytics and help customers acquire things they need, that everyone else with a newborn buys, that the new (or soon to be new) parents didn't know they needed.

Target marketing helps the seller more quickly reach their customers or reach customers that are more likely to purchase their goods and services than a "shot in the dark" hoping that someone in a particular geography may buy their products.

Case Scenario – Making Better Financial Decisions Based on Real time Information

In the financial services industry, data has helped organizations make better decisions and in a more timely manner. In investment markets, timely decision-making can make all the difference in making a decision before an investment increases as opposed to after the value of the investment has peaked. For a financial services organization that was able to gather data beyond just revenue and profitability measures, but also based on running predictive analysis on market trends, geographic trends, political climate, and consumer sentiment, the organization was able to make better investment decisions that increased success rates by over 15%.

With data at its disposal, the organization was able to calculate 15-18 different variables all in real-time, as information was gathered and made available. These multiple data points used in conjunction with historical data on similar transactions helped the organization make better decisions, more timely decisions, and more efficiently support and serve its investors.

9 BUSINESS SERVICES FOCUSED ON OPTIMIZING BUSINESS OPERATIONS

While some business services activities provide revenue generating results, other business services optimize business operations, helping organizations be more efficient in their day to day operations. This chapter continues with the case scenario format, describing real world examples of solutions that resulted in improving and optimizing business operations in enterprises.

Case Scenario – Optimizing Transactions for Cost Efficient Models

For organizations where their profit margin is extremely low, like in the grocery business, the difference of a few cents on a transaction can make all the difference whether the organization makes money or not. For many organizations on many of their goods that are transacted, there may be very little to NO profit earned on the actual sale of the product. So the way the organization makes money is to minimize their cost of transport and transaction.

It becomes a cost optimization model, where it's less about making money, it's more about cost-efficiency. Some organizations resort to decreasing costs on the frontline such as cutting employee wages or decreasing headcount. However another indirect source of cost containment is in the shipment of the product or goods.

A well-known case study is the case of Walmart Stores, that found that its trucks would drop off goods to a store or move goods across regions, but then return empty. By timing goods to return across a region so that the trucks were constantly full both coming and going, Walmart was able to increase its transport efficiencies and ultimately save money.

Walmart did this so well that many attributed the organization's profitability and success not to its role as a retailer, but as a highly efficient transport management and logistics company.

These days, organizations use this backhauling method to ensure they are efficiently and effectively optimizing their shipment operations. Even if they are able to put goods in their trucks both coming and going, many times a return haul is smaller than the initial transport, leaving a truck half empty. In these cases, logistics could contract the backhaul of a partial truckload of goods.

By monitoring the inventory loads, truck capacity, timing, and juggling the needs of contracted goods movement, organizations are able to more efficiently and effectively move materials, and in many cases make more profit in the transport of goods than in the selling of their own products.

Case Scenario – Leveraging Analytics to Optimize Social Media Outcomes

In this era of social media, the business costs and profitability may not be dependent on the selling of goods and services at all, but not losing money due to backlash on social media. Anyone monitoring the news over the past couple years has seen advertising campaigns that fell flat because of insensitivities portrayed in advertisements or some marketing campaign that didn't quite go as planned.

By doing test market analysis and sampling, the concepts of a campaign can be analyzed before costs are incurred to produce the ad or campaign. Gone are the days of being able to sample a campaign in an isolated test market as social media extends even to the smallest of markets, so a poorly thought-out localized campaign can reach national and international awareness just through the simple post of an individual in the small test market.

Organizations can take advantage of social media with benefits from "good press" and "good media outcomes" by having campaigns get more awareness and attention through reposts and retweets of materials over social media networks.

Case Scenario – Improving Healthcare Services through Real Time Communications

Data helped one healthcare network by sharing information real-time between healthcare network providers in recent cases of epidemic outbreaks of Ebola and influenza. Health outbreaks are the same no matter what region or location. The symptoms and the treatments are the same worldwide.

By leveraging knowledge gained from impacts sites, healthcare workers in other sites were already aware of what to look for. First response care, containment and control made all the difference in this healthcare network's ability to address the outbreaks.

When a patient was admitted, key signs based on previous real-world experiences helped the first line care professionals determine whether a patient's condition could be highly contagious Ebola or a common case of the cold or flu. Treatments and even the need for containment vary case to case; however information made all the difference in managing over 80% of the first response actions in a manner that resulted in more success.

Case Scenario – Utilizing Predictive Analytics to Accelerate Solution Availability

In the Biotech field, drug development is a lengthy process, sometimes taking 3, 5, even 10 years to run enough trials to validate the success of the drug. By leveraging predictive analysis tools, one Biotech firm has been able to predict the potential success of their drugs over 60% faster than before.

Rather than waiting 18-24 months on initial trials, data from early sampling indicated whether the test results were trending favorably or not, allowing the drug developer to make modifications to their product or scrap a test months before it could previously as a result of the analysis and validation.

Drug developers are very dependent on the success of their trials. The sooner they are able to determine that a drug may not be successful, the sooner they can redirect resources to the development and trial of other potentially successful outcomes. The difference of weeks and months can make the difference in funding cycles so that the organization does not run out of investment funding before it can successfully test out its product(s).

The result for several Biotech firms has meant the difference between going out of business or thriving as a result of having another few months in their development and release cycle!

10 WRAP-UP

Hopefully this book helped take you, the reader, through the journey of shifting from I.T. operations of the past into models leveraging the latest, most modern methods of business service focused operations. Executives that can think about the future, that can creatively think of new ways to leverage technology solutions are those that frame the future business operations and optimization that lead the marketplace and industry into more efficient and effective business models.

Value of Current Knowledge Not Historical Expertise

The era is gone where someone with 10 or 20 years of experience was of the most value to an organization when technologies being released today didn't exist even 2 or 3 years ago. The knowledge to administer, manage, and support modern systems is all new, and thus current knowledge is more important than years of historical expertise.

For organizations leveraging the latest built-in biometric authentication tools tied to cloud-based directory logon services that have NO tie to traditional Microsoft Active Directory logon and password services, these new tools have completely new ways of being configured, managed, and serviced. Years of Active Directory expertise with traditional domain controllers, on-premise server replication, and system management has in large part become irrelevant in managing the modern systems and models.

The individual who understands the current authentication system that just came out a year ago is the one that provides the most value to the organization for this new system. It is a complete change in how I.T. personnel value has shifted, from those with years of deep rooted knowledge and expertise, to those with experience with the current product and tools.

Importance of Institutional Knowledge

However, institutional knowledge and expertise does hold value at times. Some examples are when older technologies have to be migrated or updated to newer solutions, or when older systems have to be assessed in newer or more modern ways. When an organization is in a hybrid or transition state moving from their legacy systems to the modern systems, just knowing the new stuff gets a lot of I.T. professionals in trouble as they don't understand how or why certain things were setup or configured the way they were or even that the organization has specific policies or processes that need to be followed to effectively transition to the new environment. These are cases when institutional knowledge can be of extreme value, and that knowledge needs to be leveraged in order to retain key business system states.

Migrations tend to happen once in an enterprise, and once completed, that skill and knowledge is then of less value to the enterprise. So the I.T. professional with the institutional knowledge needs to skill-up on the new technologies, the modern methods of management, and evolve just like technologies evolve into the new methods of business operations.

Changing the Mindset to New and Creative Manners of Action

A key focus for organizations as they rapidly change from existing business models to new modern operational models is to rid itself of thinking that "we haven't done that before" or "that's not a best practice we've used in the past." Just as was covered in Chapter 5 on the value or need to backup cloud services that required a completely new way of thinking about cloud-stored data, many of the best practices of the past are no longer applicable in the current operational business.

However, best practices for the modern model many times have not been written yet, and with the velocity of the evolution of tech these days, organizations that are going to lead in the marketplace need to be the innovators developing the best practices themselves. This is where those who have years of developing institutional knowledge and best practices have an advantage. They have been involved in the development of best practices and are better positioned to create new best practices.

The new way of doing things just have to be ways applicable and appropriate to the new operational models, not just taking legacy processes and putting them in place in the new model. Moving forward, there is a dire need for best practices to be developed, and constantly evaluated and reassessed as cloud-services change with new features and functions added on a regular basis.

Shifting From Technology Focused to Business Solution Focused

This book has been about shifting I.T. from technologies to being a business services enabler. Its been about flipping around an organization's need not from "driving technology first" but to look at what the organization "needs to do" and leveraging the tools available to "make that happen".

This is the type of thinking organizations need, its best employees to rethink and redo what and how I.T. operations can be changed to enable new and better ways of providing I.T. operational services to the organization.

It's the shift from creating a business solution out of a technology to solving a business need through the use technology.

WRAP-UP

ABOUT THE AUTHORS

<u>Rand Morimoto, Ph.D.</u>: Rand has a unique blend of deep technical knowledge and expertise, and an academic background in organizational behavior and organizational management.

Rand blends the theory of business and economics with his knowledge and day to day experience in the tech industry, resulting in the content highlighted in this book.

<u>Rich Dorfman, MBA</u>: Rich has 30 years' experience in the information technology industry.

Rich' passion lies in how technology can help individuals and businesses, his contribution to the book focuses on highlighting the why and how technology is being used to contribute to business success.

www.ingramcontent.com/pod-product-compliance
Lightning Source LLC
Chambersburg PA
CBHW030050230526
45471CB00003B/1021